CONSIDERED FOR SLAUGHTER

HITLER

SUNDARAM DUBEY

Copyright © Sundaram Dubey
All Rights Reserved.

Contents

1

Hitlers rise to power

Discharged from the hospital amid the social chaos that followed Germany's defeat, Hitler took up political work in Munich in May–June 1919. As an army political agent, he joined the small German Workers' Party in Munich (September 1919). In 1920 he was put in charge of the party's propaganda and left the army to devote himself to improving his position within the party, which in that year was renamed the National-sozialistische Deutsche Arbeiterpartei (Nazi). Conditions were ripe for the development of such a party. Resentment at the loss of the war and the severity of the peace terms added to the economic woes and brought widespread discontent. This was especially sharp in Bavaria, due to its traditional separatism and the region's popular dislike of the republican government in Berlin. In March 1920 a coup d'état by a few army officers attempted in vain to establish a right-wing government.

Munich was a gathering place for dissatisfied former servicemen and members of the Freikorps, which had been organized in 1918–19 from units of the German army that were unwilling to return to civilian life, and for political plotters against the republic. Many of these joined the Nazi Party. Foremost among them was Ernst Röhm, a staff member of the district army command, who had joined the German Workers' Party before Hitler and who was of great help in furthering Hitler's rise within the party. It was he who recruited the "strong arm" squads used by Hitler to protect party meetings, to attack socialists and communists, and to exploit violence for the impression of strength it gave. In 1921 these squads were formally organized under Röhm into a private party army, the SA (Sturmabteilung). Röhm was also able to secure protection from the Bavarian government, which depended on the local army command for the maintenance of order and which tacitly accepted some of his terrorist tactics.

Conditions were favourable for the growth of the small party, and Hitler was sufficiently astute to take full advantage of them. When he joined the party, he found it ineffective, committed to a program of nationalist and socialist ideas but uncertain of its aims and divided in its leadership. He accepted its program but regarded it as a means to an end. His propaganda and his personal ambition caused friction with the other leaders of the party. Hitler countered their attempts to curb him by threatening resignation, and because the future of the party depended on his power to organize publicity and to acquire funds, his opponents relented. In July 1921 he became their leader with almost unlimited powers. From the first he set out to create a mass movement, whose mystique and power would be sufficient to bind its members in loyalty to him. He engaged in unrelenting propaganda through the party newspaper, the Völkischer Beobachter ("Popular Observer," acquired in 1920), and through meetings whose audiences soon grew from a handful to thousands. With his charismatic personality and dynamic leadership, he attracted a devoted cadre of Nazi leaders, men whose names today live in infamy—Johann Dietrich Eckart (who acted as a mentor for Hitler), Alfred Rosenberg, Rudolf Hess, Hermann Göring, and Julius Streicher.

The climax of this rapid growth of the Nazi Party in Bavaria came in an attempt to seize power in the Munich (Beer Hall) Putsch of November 1923, when Hitler and General Erich Ludendorff tried to take advantage of the prevailing confusion and opposition to the Weimar Republic to force the leaders of the Bavarian government and the local army commander to proclaim a national revolution. In the melee that resulted, the police and the army fired at the advancing marchers, killing a few of them. Hitler was injured, and four policemen were killed. Placed on trial for treason, he characteristically took advantage of the immense publicity afforded to him. He also drew a vital lesson from the Putsch—that the movement must achieve power by legal means. He was sentenced to prison for five years but served only nine months, and those in relative comfort at Landsberg castle. Hitler used the time to dictate the first volume of Mein Kampf, his political autobiography as well as a compendium of his multitudinous ideas.

Hitler's ideas included inequality among races, nations, and individuals as part of an unchangeable natural order that exalted the "Aryan race" as the creative element of mankind. According to Hitler, the natural unit of mankind was the Volk ("the people"), of which the German people was the greatest. Moreover, he believed that the state existed to serve the Volk—a mission that to him the Weimar German Republic betrayed. All morality and truth were judged by this criterion: whether it was in accordance with the interest and preservation of the Volk. Parliamentary democratic government stood doubly condemned. It assumed the equality of individuals that for Hitler did not exist and supposed that what was in the interests of the Volk could be decided by parliamentary procedures. Instead, Hitler argued that the unity of the Volk would find its incarnation in the Führer, endowed with perfect authority. Below the Führer the party was drawn from the Volk and was in turn its safeguard.

The greatest enemy of Nazism was not, in Hitler's view, liberal democracy in Germany, which was already on the verge of collapse. It was the rival Weltanschauung, Marxism (which for him embraced social democracy as well as communism), with its insistence on internationalism and economic conflict. Beyond Marxism he believed the greatest enemy of all to be the Jew, who was for Hitler the incarnation of evil. There is debate among historians as to when anti-Semitism became Hitler's deepest and strongest conviction. As early as 1919 he wrote, "Rational anti-Semitism must lead to systematic legal opposition. Its final objective must be the removal of the Jews altogether." In Mein Kampf, he described the Jew as the "destroyer of culture," "a parasite within the nation," and "a menace."

During Hitler's absence in prison, the Nazi Party languished as the result of internal dissension. After his release, Hitler faced difficulties that had not existed before 1923. Economic stability had been achieved by a currency reform and the Dawes Plan had scaled back Germany's World War I reparations. The republic seemed to have become more respectable. Hitler was forbidden to make speeches, first in Bavaria, then in many other German states (these prohibitions remained in force until 1927–28). Nevertheless, the party grew slowly in numbers, and in 1926 Hitler successfully established his position within it against Gregor Strasser, whose followers were primarily in northern Germany.

The advent of the Depression in 1929, however, led to a new period of political instability. In 1930 Hitler made an alliance with the Nationalist Alfred Hugenberg in a campaign against the Young Plan, a second renegotiation of Germany's war reparation payments. With the help of Hugenberg's newspapers, Hitler was able for the first time to reach a nationwide audience. The alliance also enabled him to seek support from many of the magnates of business and industry who controlled political funds and were anxious to use them to establish a strong right-wing, antisocialist government. The subsidies Hitler received from the industrialists placed his party on a secure financial footing and enabled him to make effective his emotional appeal to the lower middle class and the unemployed, based on the proclamation of his faith that Germany would awaken from its sufferings to reassert its natural greatness. Hitler's dealings with Hugenberg and the industrialists exemplify his skill in using those who sought to use him. But his most important achievement was the establishment of a truly national party (with its voters and followers drawn from different classes and religious groups), unique in Germany at the time.

Unremitting propaganda, set against the failure of the government to improve conditions during the Depression, produced a steadily mounting electoral strength for the Nazis. The party became the second largest in the country, rising from 2.6 percent of the vote in the national election of 1928 to more than 18 percent in September 1930. In 1932 Hitler opposed Hindenburg in the presidential election, capturing 36.8 percent of the votes on the second ballot. Finding himself in a strong position by virtue of his unprecedented mass following, he entered into a series of intrigues with conservatives such as Franz von Papen, Otto Meissner, and President Hindenburg's son, Oskar. The fear of communism and the rejection of the Social Democrats bound them together. In spite of a decline in the Nazi Party's votes in November 1932, Hitler insisted that the chancellorship was the only office he would accept. On January 30, 1933, Hindenburg offered him the chancellorship of Germany. His cabinet included few Nazis at that point.

2
Dictatorship

Once in power, Hitler established an absolute dictatorship. He secured the president's assent for new elections. The Reichstag fire, on the night of February 27, 1933 (apparently the work of a Dutch Communist, Marinus van der Lubbe), provided an excuse for a decree overriding all guarantees of freedom and for an intensified campaign of violence. In these conditions, when the elections were held (March 5), the Nazis polled 43.9 percent of the votes. On March 21 the Reichstag assembled in the Potsdam Garrison Church to demonstrate the unity of National Socialism with the old conservative Germany, represented by Hindenburg. Two days later the Enabling Bill, giving full powers to Hitler, was passed in the Reichstag by the combined votes of Nazi, Nationalist, and Centre party deputies (March 23, 1933). Less than three months later all non-Nazi parties, organizations, and labor unions ceased to exist. The disappearance of the Catholic Centre Party was followed by a German Concordat with the Vatican in July. (See Adolf Hitler addressing the Reichstag.)

Hitler had no desire to spark a radical revolution. Conservative "ideas" were still necessary if he was to succeed to the presidency and retain the support of the army; moreover, he did not intend to expropriate the leaders of industry, provided they served the interests of the Nazi state. Ernst Röhm, however, was a protagonist of the "continuing revolution"; he was also, as head of the SA, distrusted by the army. Hitler tried first to secure Röhm's support for his policies by persuasion. Hermann Göring and Heinrich Himmler were eager to remove Röhm, but Hitler hesitated until the last moment. Finally, on June 29, 1934, he reached his decision. On the "Night of the Long Knives," Röhm and his lieutenant Edmund Heines were executed without trial, along with Gregor Strasser, Kurt von Schleicher, and others.

The army leaders, satisfied at seeing the SA broken up, approved Hitler's actions. When Hindenburg died on August 2, the army leaders, together with Papen, assented to the merging of the chancellorship and the presidency—with which went the supreme command of the armed forces of the Reich. Now officers and men took an oath of allegiance to Hitler personally. Economic recovery and a fast reduction in unemployment (coincident with world recovery, but for which Hitler took credit) made the regime increasingly popular, and a combination of success and police terror brought the support of 90 percent of the voters in a plebiscite.

Hitler devoted little attention to the organization and running of the domestic affairs of the Nazi state. Responsible for the broad lines of policy, as well as for the system of terror that upheld the state, he left detailed administration to his subordinates. Each of these exercised arbitrary power in his own sphere; but by deliberately creating offices and organizations with overlapping authority, Hitler effectively prevented any one of these particular realms from ever becoming sufficiently strong to challenge his own absolute authority.

Foreign policy claimed his greater interest. As he had made clear in Mein Kampf, the reunion of the German peoples was his overriding ambition. Beyond that, the natural field of expansion lay eastward, in Poland, the Ukraine, and the U.S.S.R.—expansion that would necessarily involve renewal of Germany's historic conflict with the Slavic peoples, who would be subordinate in the new order to the Teutonic master race. He saw fascist Italy as his natural ally in this crusade. Britain was a possible ally, provided that it would abandon its traditional policy of maintaining the balance of power in Europe and limit itself to its interests overseas. In the west France remained the natural enemy of Germany and must, therefore, be cowed or subdued to make expansion eastward possible.

Before such expansion was possible, it was necessary to remove the restrictions placed on Germany at the end of World War I by the Treaty of Versailles. Hitler used all the arts of propaganda to allay the suspicions of the other powers. He posed as the champion of Europe against the scourge of Bolshevism and insisted that he was a man of peace who wished only to remove the inequalities of the Versailles Treaty. He withdrew from the Disarmament Conference and from the League of Nations (October 1933), and he signed a nonaggression treaty with Poland (January 1934). Every repudiation of the treaty was followed by an offer to negotiate a fresh agreement and insistence on the limited nature of Germany's ambitions.

4

The hate for jews

In January 1933, some 522,000 Jews by religious definition lived in Germany. Over half of these individuals, approximately 304,000 Jews, emigrated during the first six years of the Nazi dictatorship, leaving only approximately 214,000 Jews in Germany proper (1937 borders) on the eve of World War II.

In the years between 1933 and 1939, the Nazi regime had brought radical and daunting social, economic, and communal change to the German Jewish community. Six years of Nazi-sponsored legislation had marginalized and disenfranchised Germany's Jewish citizenry and had expelled Jews from the professions and from commercial life. By early 1939, only about 16 percent of Jewish breadwinners had steady employment of any kind. Thousands of Jews remained interned in concentration camps following the mass arrests in the aftermath of Kristallnacht (Night of the Broken Glass) in November 1938.

5

Jews after the era of hitler

With more than 200,000 people and counting, Germany's Jewish community is the only one in Europe with a rapidly increasing population — a surprising reality given the near-complete extermination of Jews within Germany during the Holocaust.

Today's growing numbers are even more remarkable given that in 1945 most of the world's Jews considered the idea of rebuilding their ruined communities — on the very soil where Hitler plotted and carried out a genocide — to be unthinkable.

About 15,000 German Jews were liberated by the Allied forces after the war; most of them had survived in hiding, others in concentration camps. Many of those who stayed had a non-Jewish spouse or parent who connected them to the country and perhaps facilitated recovery and integration to some degree.

'The history of Jews in Germany has found its end'

The German Jewish journalist Karl Marx — namesake of the famous German philosopher and economist — had fled into exile during the war, and was one of the first Jews to return. But the difficulty of that choice weighed on him. He recalled later that, upon crossing into the British-occupied zone in 1946, he asked himself: "How can I possibly, after all that has happened, live in Germany as a Jew?" The choice made by Marx and a few thousand other idealists like him was questioned by many both within and outside the Jewish community.

The World Jewish Congress held its first postwar gathering in July 1948, at which it passed a resolution clearly expressing "the determination of the Jewish people never again to settle on the bloodstained soil of Germany."

It was a stand backed even by the elite of German Jews, including Leo Baeck, a leading rabbi who emigrated to London after surviving the Theresienstadt concentration camp. "The history of Jews in Germany has found its end. It is impossible for it to come back. The chasm is too great," he said just after the war ended.

Baeck remained in London, although he actively supported the rebuilding of Jewish communities in Germany throughout the late 1940s and visited the country on several occasions. In 1953, President Theodor Heuss awarded him the Order of Merit of the Federal Republic of Germany, one of country's most prominent honors, for his work.

In 1955, the international Leo Baeck Institute, devoted to the history and culture of German-speaking Jews, was named after him, and he served as its first president.

Reestablishing German Jewry against all odds

Those who chose to stay and make Germany their home despite the protestations of the much larger international Jewish community had many different reasons, said Anthony Kauders, a history professor at the UK's Keele University. "Some of those who stayed had survived with the help of non-Jewish Germans, and they refused to see all Germans equally culpable. Others were simply too old or too frail to migrate," he said.

hey were made up of two very distinct groups: There were the German-born Jews, most of whom had been highly assimilated and connected with their German surroundings. On the other side were thousands of displaced Jewish refugees from Eastern European countries who found themselves unwillingly in Germany. With limited means and limited knowledge of the German language, they struggled to find permanent living solutions.

More than 90% of the Jewish refugees who had ended up in Germany left within three to four years, mostly to the US and the newly founded state of Israel. Only about 15,000 of them stayed on German soil. "Some of them found jobs very quickly and they simply made a living," said Kauders. "Staying in the beginning was to certain extent ad hoc, and it came to be permanent."

Many of those Eastern European Jews eventually became naturalized Germans. New to the country, they relied on the community as a support system for their religious, social and cultural needs. "They led very secluded lives," said Kauders. "In the '50s and '60s, as a member of the Jewish community, the only people you really know were other Jews, and you don't mix with others too much."

In July 1950 the disparate communities joined forces and established an umbrella organization to represent them: The Central Council of Jews in Germany.

The defiant insistence of the German Jewish community led to pragmatic cooperation from the international Jewish institutions. "While it was the opinion and policy of the World Jewish Congress that Jews should leave Germany, those who chose to stay in Germany would be gladly given advice," the WJC said upon the German Central Council's founding. By 1954, the WJC and several other international Jewish organizations had become affiliated with the German body.

Anti-Semitism, meanwhile, continued to be pervasive in Germany. A December 1946 report on anti-Semitism circulated by the US Army found that 18% of Germans were still "radical anti-Semites," 21% were "anti-Semites" and another 22% were "moderate racists." A poll from 1947 found that more than one-third of all Germans felt that it was better for there to be no Jews in Germany.

Attacks on synagogues in Germany

The attempted attack on a synagogue in Halle is not the first in recent years. Even after the horrors of the Nazi era, anti-Semitic incidents occur in Germany — on individuals, memorials and Jewish places of worship.

In December 1959, two members of the Deutsche Reichspartei (DRP) right-wing extremist party painted swastikas and the words "Germans demand: Jews out" on the synagogue in Cologne. Anti-Semitic graffiti emerged across the country. The perpetrators were convicted, and the Bundestag passed a law against "incitement of the people," which remains on the books to this day.

People across the world were horrified at the March 1994 attack on the synagogue in the northern city of Lübeck. For the first time in decades, a synagogue in Germany burned. Four right-wing extremists were eventually convicted of arson. The day after the fire, 4,000 locals took to the streets under the slogan "Lübeck holds its breath." In 1995, the same synagogue was hit by another arson attack.

Armed with paving stones, more than 100 Palestinians from Lebanon attacked the Old Synagogue in Essen in October 2000. The incident occurred after a demonstration against "violence in the Middle East." A police officer was injured. Mahmud Alaeddin, deputy head of the general delegation of Palestine in Germany, distanced himself from the attack.

A 19-year-old Palestinian and a 20-year-old Moroccan damaged Düsseldorf's New Synagogue with incendiary devices and rocks in October 2000 as "revenge" against Jews and the state of Israel. "We need the respectable people to rebel" against anti-Semitism, then-German Chancellor Gerhard Schröder demanded. The federal and state governments and various NGOs launched campaigns to counter extremism.

Shortly after being inaugurated in September 2010, an arson attack hit the New Synagogue in Mainz during the night of October 30. The spectacular Deconstructivist building by architect Manuel Herz was erected on the site of the former main synagogue that was set on fire during the Kristallnacht, the Nazis' national night of pogroms, in 1938.

In July 2014, three young Palestinians hurled incendiary devices at the front door of the synagogue in Wuppertal. In a highly controversial decision, the court ruled there was "no evidence whatsoever" of anti-Semitic motives. Jews in Germany and the foreign media were outraged. The chairman of the Jewish Community Wuppertal declared the ruling as "an invitation to further crimes."

A man wielding a knife climbed over a barrier at Berlin's New Synagogue on the eve of Shabbat on October 4, 2019, during the holy period between the holidays of Rosh Hashanah and Yom Kippur. Security personnel overwhelmed the attacker, whose motive remained unclear. Police released him afterwards, a decision Jewish leaders called "a failure" of justice.

About 80 people were in the synagogue on Wednesday afternoon to observe Yom Kippur, the Jewish calendar's holiest day. The alleged attacker reportedly attempted to shoot his way into the synagogue but was prevented by a safety door. Two passersby were shot to death and two were injured. The suspect, who has a history of right-wing extremist, anti-Semitic, and misogynist rhetoric, was detained.